Pebble® Plus

LET'S LOOK AT COUNTRIES

LET'S LOOK AT
RUSSIA

NIKKI BRUNO CLAPPER

raintree

a Capstone company — publishers for children

Raintree is an imprint of Capstone Global Library Limited, a company incorporated in England and Wales having its registered office at 264 Banbury Road, Oxford, OX2 7DY – Registered company number: 6695582

www.raintree.co.uk
myorders@raintree.co.uk

Text © Capstone Global Library Limited 2019
The moral rights of the proprietor have been asserted.

Edited by Carrie Sheely
Designed by Juliette Peters
Picture research by Tracy Cummins
Production by Laura Manthe
Originated by Capstone Global Library Limited
Printed and bound in India

ISBN 978 1 4747 5308 1 (hardback)
22 21 20 19 18
10 9 8 7 6 5 4 3 2 1

ISBN 978 1 4747 5314 2 (paperback)
22 21 20 19 18
10 9 8 7 6 5 4 3 2 1

British Library Cataloguing in Publication Data
A full catalogue record for this book is available from the British Library.

Acknowledgements
We would like to thank the following for permission to reproduce photographs: Dreamstime: Mengtianhan, 16-17; iStockphoto: Pro-syanov, 13; Shutterstock: Aleksandr Kutskii, 10, Boris Rezvantsev, Cover Bottom, Ekaterina Bykova, 21, EvgenySHCH, 5, Katvic, 9, KUSHELEV IVAN, Cover Top, Martin Mecnarowski, 11, mutee meesa, 22 Top, nale, 4, NaumB, Cover Middle, Cover Back, Nikitin Victor, 6–7, Pavel L Photo and Video, 14, Tatiana Grozetskaya, 3, Timolina, 19, Viacheslav Lopatin, 1, 22–23, 24, vladimir salman, 15

Every effort has been made to contact copyright holders of material reproduced in this book. Any omissions will be rectified in subsequent printings if notice is given to the publisher.

All the internet addresses (URLs) given in this book were valid at the time of going to press. However, due to the dynamic nature of the internet, some addresses may have changed, or sites may have changed or ceased to exist since publication. While the author and publisher regret any inconvenience this may cause readers, no responsibility for any such changes can be accepted by either the author or the publisher.

CONTENTS

Where is Russia?

Russia is the largest country in the world. It is in Europe and Asia. Russia is almost twice as big as the United States. Its capital is Moscow.

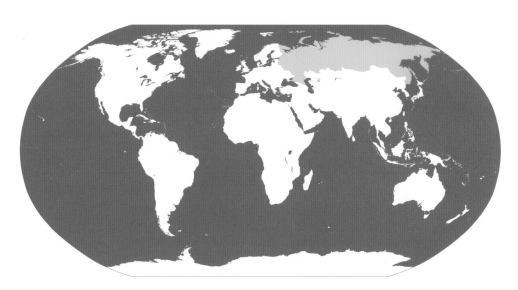

■ Russia

From forest to tundra

Forests cover half of Russia.

In the north is frozen tundra.

The Ural Mountains stretch

north to south. Russia also

has plains and marshes.

Russia has thousands of rivers and lakes. Lake Baikal is the world's deepest lake. It is about 1.6 kilometres (1 mile) deep.

In the wild

Bears and Siberian tigers
roam Russian forests.
Snow leopards hunt
in the mountains.
Musk oxen live in the tundra.

musk oxen

Siberian tiger

People

Many groups of people live in Russia. Most are Slavic. Other people include Tatars, Ukrainians and Bashkirs.

At work

Many Russians build machines, cars or ships. Others help people. They include nurses, teachers and food servers.

At the ballet

Russia is famous for ballet. Many great ballet dancers are Russian. Dancers leap and spin. They perform at theatres in big cities.

At the table

Russians eat a lot of

soup, cabbage and fish.

Borscht is beetroot soup.

It is served with sour cream.

borscht

A famous site

The Kremlin is a group

of buildings in Moscow.

It includes churches and palaces.

Russia's president lives there.

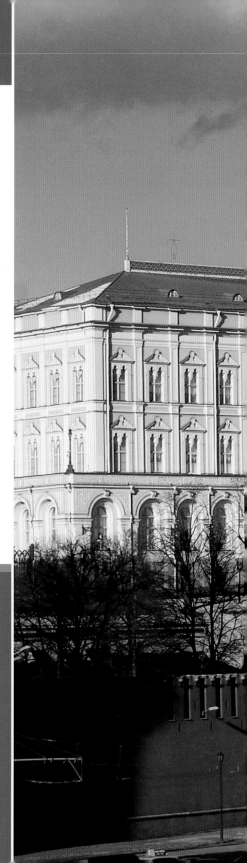

QUICK RUSSIA FACTS

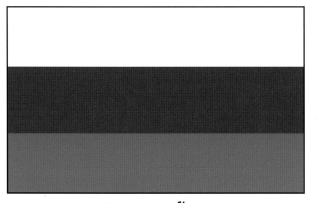

Russian flag

Name: Russian Federation

Capital: Moscow

Other major cities: St. Petersburg, Novosibirsk, Yekaterinburg

Population: 142,355,415 (July 2016 estimate)

Size: 17,075,400 square km (6,592,850 sq mi)

Language: Russian

Money: ruble

GLOSSARY

ballet performance that uses dance to tell a story

capital city in a country where the government is based

marsh area of wet, low land usually covered in grasses and plants

plain large, flat area with few trees

president highest elected job in a class, business or country

tundra cold area of northern Europe, Asia and North America where trees do not grow; the ground stays frozen in the tundra for most of the year

FIND OUT MORE

BOOKS

Russia: A Benjamin Blog and His Inquisitive Dog Guide (Country Guides, with Benjamin Blog and His Inquisitive Dog), Anita Ganeri (Raintree, 2015)

Let's Explore Russia (Let's Explore Countries), Walt K. Moon (Bumba Books, 2017)

Life in a Tundra (Biomes Alive!), Kari Schuetz (Bellwether Media, 2016)

WEBSITES

http://www.natgeokids.com/uk/discover/geography/countries/russia-facts/
Learn about the world's largest country.

http://www.bbc.co.uk/education/clips/zcsdtfr
Listen to music from the famous Russian ballet, *The Nutcracker.*

http://www.bbc.co.uk/nature/life/Siberian_Crane
Learn about a rare bird found only in Russia.

COMPREHENSION QUESTIONS

1. What types of land does Russia have?

2. Look at the photo on page 10. What features do musk oxen have that might help them live in the cold tundra?

3. Look at the photo on page 21. Why do you think there is a wall around the Kremlin?

INDEX